angel hike

D1521872

angel hike

an answer to prayer about Alzheimer's

a novel by
brian rihner

TATE PUBLISHING & *Enterprises*

dedication

To my wife, Lynne—you are always there for me, always faithful, always thinking of everyone except yourself.

To my kids, Marcus, Kevin, and Alyssa—it's great that we really do enjoy our time together. May you continue to grow strong in the Lord.

To my Dad—thanks for being there for Mom all those years.

To my Mom—your life was cut too short. May the promises brought out in this book help others as much as they helped all of us through your illness.

introduction

I remember the first time I sat at the bedside of an Alzheimer's patient as a student chaplain in Austin, Texas. I felt out of place and so useless. What was I supposed to do for this person who only mumbled a few seemingly meaningless phrases every five minutes or so? His eyes rarely opened. He didn't know who I was or what I was doing there. He didn't know his children anymore. He didn't even know his own wife.

It is because of times like this that I wrote *Angel Hike*. I have been at the bedside of many people in different stages of Alzheimer's, other forms of dementia, or who have suffered a massive stroke. Our faith in Christ is certainly tested at times like this. The questions from family and friends are heartfelt and sincere: "Why is this happening?" "Where is God in all of this?"

As I entered into full-time parish ministry those same questions kept coming. I struggled to give an answer, to give real comfort and hope. I resolved to help people in these situations. I began doing the same thing I did at the bedside of that man in Texas, the same thing we are all asked to do when we don't understand and we think we have nothing to offer—

I prayed. I searched the Bible for help and meaning. And slowly, sometimes at very unexpected times, I received insight, comfort, and even a little bit of understanding. Almost all of this insight came directly from the Bible. It was always there but I often failed to understand it completely, or worse yet, I thought I had already exhausted its meaning in other ways.

This book contains some of those insights. The characters are all fictional, even the angel. Maybe I should say *especially* the angel. I have never seen an angel, as far as I know. I doubt I ever will. My belief is that we are to be faithful to our Lord, to turn to Him in prayer, to search His word, to ask for His guidance and direction, and to let Him work out the method. As you read this book, I encourage you to look closely at what the angel says, how he says it, and what is of importance to him.

One potential danger of writing a book like this is that people will look for their own "angel experience." If that is what the endgame of this book becomes, I have failed in my main purpose. My hope is that this book encourages people to get on their knees in prayer to God, and to open their Bibles for answers and discernment.

The characters in this book may be fictional, but they struggle with real issues. Alzheimer's, other forms of dementia, and strokes are very hard to deal with. They are very real and they are becoming more prevalent each day in our world. Ultimately, my hope and prayer is that this book will help any of you who may be dealing with a situation that is similar to this fictional family. May you turn to the One who truly cares and who alone can give you true peace and ultimate comfort.

"I have told you these things, so that in me you may have

peace. In this world you will have trouble. But take heart! I have overcome the world." John 16:33 (NIV)

IXS,

Rev. Brian Rihner

chapter 1

Ben split the last three logs and threw the pieces into the back of the pickup. The snowfall became more intense as he tied down the tarp. "Not much chance of this heavy hickory falling out, but if we're going to have a good fire tonight the wood can't be wet," he said out loud, mostly to himself, but partially to Gabe, his eight-year-old chocolate Lab.

Ben opened the truck door and Gabe jumped into his familiar spot on the passenger side. "Seems like in the last two years you get that spot more than just about anyone else in the family," Ben said as he rubbed Gabe's head and put the key into the ignition.

The old pickup roared to life on the first try, just like always. *Too bad people don't always hold up with age so well*, Ben thought as he put the truck in gear and headed west hoping to get to the cabin before the rest of the family showed up.

———————

Barb wrung the water out of the wash cloth and placed it on her dad's head as the nurse poked her head in the door. "Can I get you two anything?" the nurse said in a whisper. "It's lunch time and I know Jake has the IV, but do you want to try to give him something soft, or would you like something yourself?"

"Oh, no thanks, I think we're fine," Barb replied, but then changed her mind. "Maybe some chocolate pudding?"

Dad always liked chocolate pudding, Barb thought, although in his present condition he probably wouldn't enjoy it quite as much as he used to. His fever had been hanging on for almost a week and he slept most of the time now. She remembered how strong he once was, how he used to have all three of them hanging from one arm after he came home from work. She remembered the wrestling matches—three against one—but he always had enough strength and grace to never let any of them bump heads or land on each other, although each one got a turn to land on the couch after a flight through the air.

Barb stared at her dad and a tear came to her eye. *Now look at him*, she thought, asleep most of the time, hardly able to recognize any of his kids or the grandkids. *Why this way God? He was so full of life. I don't understand.* Her head sank down to his shoulder as her heart ached for an answer, for some peace in all of this. Suddenly she raised her head and looked at the clock on the wall—12:15 p.m. In the hours taking care of her dad she lost track of time…again. *Hadn't the nurse just been in here telling you it was lunch time?* she thought to herself. *I still have to get the food for the trip and pack and pick up the kids from school, and I'm already running over an hour late.*

"See you later, Dad," Barb said as she took the wash cloth off of his head and placed it in the water. "I'll be back to see you on Monday, but Claire will be by over the weekend." But, as was customary for the last month or so, no response.

Barb hardly noticed the heavy snow as she left the care center for her SUV, "So much to do and so little time," she murmured to herself.

"Come on Natalie! You have to come to my birthday party this weekend. You're my best friend!" Sheila tried one more desperate attempt to convince her to change her mind.

"It's not really an option for me you know," Natalie replied. And she was right. The family had been going to the cabin in mid-February since before she was born. *David was a year older and he never complained about the three day vacation in the middle of nowhere*, she thought.

"Sheila, you know I would love to stay here and go to your party, but my family has done this annual 'cabin-thing' for, like, twenty years or so. And your real birthday was two weeks ago."

"Yeah, and now I can drive! And your trip…it just sounds so boring."

"It's not so bad when you get up there. And it means a lot to Mom and Dad, and my brothers."

"But, guys like that kind of stuff up in the woods with no TV, no Internet; at least you'll have your cell phone."

"No signal," Natalie replied as Sheila's mom pulled up in a huge SUV.

"I guess I'll get to finally talk to you on Monday then. Say hello to the wolves," Sheila said as she opened the car door.

"Have a great party," Natalie replied. She blurted out a "Wish I could be there!" as she gave a weak wave and smile.

Natalie sat back down on the bench and waited for her

ride. She still had three months to go before she would turn sixteen and get her license. *A little bit of freedom*, she thought. But she knew that that "freedom" would include picking up Liz from school every day. Mom hardly had time with her part time job and with taking care of Grandpa. Her mind wandered to the many weekends at the cabin—Mom, Dad, David, Liz, Greg, Grandpa Jake, Grandma Liz, and of course Gabe. It changed quite a bit when Grandma passed away five years ago, but now with Grandpa in this condition, "Why do we bother?" Natalie said out loud to no one in particular. "And where's Mom?" she said as she tightened her scarf to keep the falling snow from going down her neck.

chapter 2

The engine of the old pickup finally stopped a good five seconds after Ben took the key out of the ignition. *I've got to take a look at that carburetor again,* he thought, although he knew that his auto mechanic ability was extremely limited.

He thought back to the first time he had looked underneath the hood of the truck. He and Barb had just purchased it from a shady used car dealer and it had barely made it up her parents' driveway. *But Jake was so gracious about the whole thing,* Ben thought. *We had only been married three months. I bet he thought, "What a yahoo—this guy marries my daughter and can't even provide decent transportation." Well if he thought that, he sure never showed it. Two hours after we bought the truck Jake had it running like a new one, and it had run well ever since—until now.*

How ironic, Ben thought, *the old truck starts running down right after Dad.* Ben paused to think about that word—Dad. He started calling Jake that less than a year after he and Barb were married. Since his dad was killed when he was three, he never really knew what it was like to have a dad, but in the last twenty years Jake had certainly been the father Ben never had. He could easily see how Barb looked up to him so much. Strong, caring, bright, and hilarious; "But where is that now?" Ben said out loud, partially as a real question, but mostly in anger.

Ben finished bringing in the firewood and searched the cabin for matches or a lighter. A few dried leaves and five or six paper towels worked well as a starter, and in no time the dry hickory was crackling to life. He went outside one last time to put the tarp away and noticed that the moderate snow fall had changed into more of a blizzard. Ben's thoughts turned to Barb and the kids…

Barb pulled into the driveway with Natalie and Liz. More than an hour at the grocery store had left them all in a bad mood. She saw David's Escort in the carport. Hopefully he had remembered to pick up Greg from basketball practice at the elementary.

"Did you remember Greg?" she said as she saw David's feet on the couch through the doorway.

"Oh yeah, I thought there was something I was supposed to do," David shot back.

"We were supposed to leave for the cabin twenty minutes ago and I haven't even finished packing! How could you forget?" Barb shouted.

Just then Greg came running into the kitchen to look through the grocery bag for candy.

"David!"

Almost an hour later Barb and all four kids were in the

Excursion and on their way to the mountains, but traffic was very slow—the snow was not.

"I don't understand why I can't drive," David said for the fifth time.

Barb looked at him and rolled her eyes, "You've got less than two years of driving experience. You think this is a good time to test your skills?"

Natalie's nose was buried in a book while listening to her iPod. The younger two were watching a DVD. The snow was coming down hard and the wind was blowing. Barb kept her eyes glued to the red taillights immediately ahead of her. She started digging through her purse for her cell phone, but gave up as she realized there was no use—no signal at the cabin. *Dad and Gabe might be the only ones staying at the cabin tonight...*

chapter 3

Ben finished up the last few green beans on his plate and tossed Gabe the final piece of steak. He had hoped that the whole family could enjoy this steak meal together, but he knew that there was no way Barb would venture up the mountain in this snow, and he wouldn't want her to. Hopefully the snow would quit soon and the roads could get cleared off enough for them to join him tomorrow. *The cross-country skiing trails should be just about right*, he thought, *if the snow could just lighten up a bit.*

Ben went over to the stove and started the burner to warm up the coffee. This was another trait he'd picked up from Jake. If you wanted something to drink at the cabin it was either water or coffee. Coffee was about the only thing that Jake drank or ate that wasn't really good for him.

"I never would have dreamed that a strong man like that would end up dying like this..." Ben's words trailed off as he continued to rub Gabe's head. His thoughts went to his father-in-law, who at this very moment, was lying in a bed that was not his own, unable to communicate with anyone beyond a few short unintelligible words at a time. *The whole thing just doesn't make sense. It doesn't seem fair.*

"God, why?" Ben caught himself saying out loud. "I know you probably think I'm an annoying whiner because this is about all I ever pray about anymore, but if I could just get some sort of reason, even a little direction. Show me some purpose for Jake to be stripped of all of his life and dignity while still…while still…living—if you can call it that. I know Jake believes in your power to heal, and Barb certainly does. I guess I do too, or I wouldn't be praying right now. But sometimes it just doesn't make sense and sometimes I wonder if you really even hear me, or have time to. Help our family. We are all struggling with this. Amen."

"Greg, I can't do anything about the weather! We'll just have to stay in a hotel tonight and try to get to the cabin in the morning," Barb yelled to the back of the SUV in an attempt to get her persistent, and disappointed, nine-year-old boy to stop complaining.

"God can change the weather," Greg blurted out, not taking the hint very well.

"Well then take it up with Him," Barb replied as she pulled into an open parking space next to the hotel entrance.

All five of them rolled out of the car and scurried various directions, Natalie and Liz to the women's bathroom, Greg to the men's, and Barb and David to the front counter.

"Can we get a room for five tonight?" Barb inquired with a smile.

"All I have left is two rooms; each has one king size bed.

One smoking. One non-smoking," the clerk replied without looking up.

"Could we get a cot?"

"That'll be ten dollars extra."

"Fine. What time is checkout?"

"11:00 a.m. Continental Breakfast starts at 6:30 a.m."

"How long is the pool open?"

"Pool's broken. Sorry."

"Great..." Barb mumbled as she took the keys and started looking for the other three kids. *I hope you're having a nice, quiet evening at the cabin, Ben*, she thought, *because my evening will be anything but quiet.*

chapter 4

Ben woke with a start because of the bright light. *Have I been sleeping that long?* he thought as he started to reach for the clock on the other side of the couch. But he could not find the clock. In fact he wasn't even on the couch.

"What the…" Ben stopped in mid sentence as he looked up to see a very tall figure standing above him. Ben noticed the man was wearing sandals and some sort of tunic with a belt around his waist, but what he really noticed was his size—well over seven feet tall and muscular. Ben thought of running but couldn't move. He sat there frozen in a mixture of fear and confusion.

"Do not be afraid, Ben," the huge man said when he finally spoke. "I am here for your benefit, and for the benefit of your family."

Without taking his eyes off of the man, Ben slowly stood up. At 6'3" Ben didn't look up to many people, but this guy was well over a foot taller than he was. "Who are you?" he finally blurted out.

"My name is unimportant."

"How did you get in here?"

"The door was unlocked, was it not?" The man's voice was deep and low, almost baritone, but very distinct, and, very…calming.

"Yeah, I guess it was, but with all the snow I didn't expect company," Ben replied.

For a moment Ben found himself staring into the man's eyes. They were a deep bluish-grey that seemed to change color with every passing moment. There was something of meaning in those eyes, some sort of depth that he had never seen before. Ben suddenly realized he was staring and looked away. He then spoke, partly in curiosity, partly in fear, and partly in anger. "What the heck are you doing here?"

"I am a messenger sent to you. But not only with a message. I have been instructed to listen to your questions for a short time. Some I will be able to answer, some will be beyond your comprehension, some are even too deep for me to understand."

"Are you an…angel?"

"In some fashion, yes. I am a messenger and an answerer sent from the one true God."

"Whoa. So I'm dreaming?"

"Yes and no."

"What do you mean, 'Yes and no?'"

"The fact that you can see me is a gift. The ability to converse with me is an extremely rare and precious opportunity that very few humans receive. Use it wisely."

"So…then am I dreaming or not?"

"What does it matter?"

"Well, is this real?"

"It is very real. More real than you can imagine. Some

call it 'dreaming,' others a 'vision.' Everyone experiences it differently. And there will always be the temptation for you to question its reality."

"Will I remember our conversation?"

"I do not know what or how much you will remember, or in what form."

"But I would have to recall some of this, or why bother?"

"That is true."

"So why me? Why now?"

"You were selected. I do not know why or how."

"Selected for what?"

"You were just praying before you fell asleep, and you have been praying for a long time about something. Have you not?"

Ben thought, and then whispered, "Jake."

chapter 5

"Liz is touching me," Greg yelled as he attempted to move closer to the edge of the bed. Barb decided to ignore him as she listened to the 10:15 p.m. weather report. The snow was expected to stop by midnight, but the roads were not expected to be clear until later tomorrow, especially the mountain roads. *We'll have to decide by eleven tomorrow morning whether to try to make it to the cabin or not*, she thought to herself.

Just then she heard her cell phone start playing "You're the Inspiration" by Chicago.

"When are you going to get a cool ringtone, Mom?" Natalie teased as she handed the phone to Barb. Barb just smiled and grabbed it. Natalie always teased her mom about having that song on her phone, but deep down it made her feel a sense of security every time she heard it. She knew it was her mom and dad's "song" from when they were first dating, and somehow admired her mom for putting it on her phone, and her dad for tolerating it.

"No we haven't made it up there yet," Barb spoke into the phone.

"Yes, he's already up there—probably bored to death."

"Why are you worried about Ben?"

"What do you mean *a feeling*?"

"Okay. Yes. I promise!"

"Love you too. Say hi to Dad. Bye."

"Who was that?" Natalie asked as she blew on the fingernails she had just painted.

"It was Aunt Claire."

"Was she calling because she was 'worried' about us?"

"Now, be nice. She worries because she cares. But she was actually calling about your dad."

"Why Dad?"

"She said she feels that we should be praying for him."

"Why? Has something happened to Dad?"

"No honey. Aunt Claire just thinks it would be nice if we would keep him in our prayers since he's up on the snowy mountain all alone."

"Kids. Let's turn the TV down and try to get some sleep. And everyone say their prayers, and remember to pray for Dad who's all alone up at the cabin tonight."

"And Grandpa," Liz added.

"And Grandpa," Barb replied.

Ben stood there for a moment trying to gather his senses. "So you are a being from God, sent to answer my questions, because I have been praying a long time about my father-in-law's Alzheimer's?"

"That is partly true."

"What do you mean *partly*?"

"I am not here because of your prayers alone. Many in

your family have been lifting their hearts to God in regards to this matter. You were chosen."

"Well, why now? What took so long?"

"I was detained."

"How? By whom?"

"There are other forces, real forces that sometimes hinder my ability to carry out my orders."

"But you're an angel! Who the heck could hinder you?"

"Ben. You do not read your Bible enough."

"What do you mean?"

"Have you ever read the book of Daniel?"

"Yeah. I suppose. A long time ago. I mostly keep to the New Testament when I read the Bible now."

"The New is deeper when the Old is understood."

"Huh?"

"The *New* is deeper when the *Old* is understood."

"But it gets so long and boring and hard to understand."

"How can reading God's revelation to you be boring?"

"Well all those rules and genealogies are hard to tread through. But some of the stories are cool."

"So you only want to read what is *cool*?"

"Well I want to read what is relevant to my life. I mean, why should I care who begat who, or what the punishment was for accidentally injuring somebody's ox?"

"So your purpose in reading the Bible is to find relevance in your life?"

"Well yeah. Is there something wrong with that?"

"No. But it is not the main thing."

"Main thing?"

"The main purpose."

"So what is?"

"Knowledge of God."

Ben started to question again, but stood silent for a moment to gather his thoughts. "So I should read the Old Testament to find knowledge about God?"

"Primarily, yes."

"But doesn't it make more sense to focus on Jesus to understand what God is like?"

"Oh yes. That is true. But knowing the scriptures that Jesus read will help you understand Him better also. It again comes back to the knowledge of God."

"I guess I really never thought about it that way. I thought since Jesus is the focal point, the Old Testament was not really necessary anymore."

"You are not the first to think in such a way. And you are correct, the Son is the focal point. All, either Old or New, point to Him."

"So what does the book of Daniel have to do with all of this?"

"In it the angel Gabriel was resisted in coming to Daniel for twenty-one days because of evil forces. I have experienced something similar."

"You were detained from coming here because of the devil?"

"Something like that."

"Well, how does that work? How did you get here then?"

"You may ask those questions, but those I can not answer. That is not why I am here."

"It sure seems very…mysterious."

"It is."

The conversation paused and Ben noticed that he was still in his cabin, everything looked as it did before he fell asleep, and this being looked more real now than before. "So I can start asking you questions about Jake?"

"Not quite yet."

"When then?"

"We must go on a walk for you to ask your deepest questions."

"A walk? Why?"

"It will help."

"Help your answers?"

"No. It will help your questions."

"Okay. Let me go get my coat. I can try to scrounge one up for you too."

"There will be no need."

"But it's freezing out there, and snowing. I would think even an angel would…" Ben stopped in mid-sentence as he noticed something he did not see before. The angel's robe was much longer than he first recollected, and it had a hood. His feet were still in sandals, but there was some sort of lining or covering over his feet that he had not noticed before. Ben went into the closet and got out his coat, gloves, and hat, and put them on, "Ready if you are…"

chapter 6

David slid quietly out from under his covers and tiptoed toward the bathroom, almost completely closing the door he flipped on the bathroom light and located his shoes and shirt. He then quietly grabbed a room key, switched off the bathroom light, avoided the cot, and slowly eased his way out of the hotel room door.

He glanced at his watch—2:45 a.m. He had been laying there for over three hours not able to sleep. Why *do I keep having all these thoughts about Dad?* he thought. *And Grandpa?* David quietly worked his way down the three flights of stairs and started to head for the front door thinking a long walk might be a good way to clear his head. But looking outside into the drifts of snow made him think otherwise, *I guess I'll have to find another way to clear my head.*

As the two headed out of the cabin door Gabe followed closely behind. The snow had subsided to a flurry and a few stars could be seen through the clouds. Ben led the angel through the dense evergreens on the north side of the cabin and onto the trail that led up to Mystery Peak. As they came into a clearing Ben started the conversation with a question. "Isn't there something I can call you? I mean, I know you said it wasn't important, but it's kind of awkward."

"At this time I am known as Apokrin."

"Apokrin it is then. At least I can pronounce it. You know I've never really had a lot of trouble with the truthfulness of God's word or that he cares about me and my family. But what I have always had trouble with, and especially now, is accidents and illnesses that seem to be so arbitrary. There doesn't seem to be any rhyme or reason for much of what happens to people in this world."

Ben paused to allow a reply but did not get one. They came through a line of poplar trees and began heading west along a rocky ridge that formed the base of the peak. He continued. "Diseases of the mind are even harder to handle. With a physical disease you can often function in some capacity. And you can get a grip on dealing with them because you can see the problem right in front of you. But when it's someone's mind, well, that seems even crueler. You have no idea how to help, no idea how to react, and very little ability to cope."

After a long pause, Apokrin spoke. "They are elusive, but not so different from what you call physical as you might think."

"What do you mean 'what you call physical?'"

"One of the great human misconceptions is that the spirit and the body are completely separate entities. They are not as separate as many have believed. What is physical and what is spiritual is not so easy to categorize, or even define. And trying to is really missing the point."

"So you're saying that there is really no difference between what is physical and what is spiritual?"

"No. There are differences, but not so much in kind as in degree."

"I think I'm confused."

"Physically confused or spiritually confused?"

"Both!"

"I was joking, but confusion is a decent example of how what is physical and what is spiritual are not only hard to categorize, they are hard to define. But again, defining them is not really the goal."

"Back to your earlier assertion—you believe that dealing with what you called a physical disease is easier than dealing with a mental one."

"For the most part, yes. I had an uncle who was bound to a wheelchair when I was growing up. He had very limited mobility, and his condition steadily got worse, but he could always talk to people, tell them what he was feeling, what he wanted, what he needed, what his hopes still were."

"So he could still communicate."

"Yeah. That's the difference. How do you continue a relationship with someone you can't talk to?"

"Now that is a deep and profound question, perhaps even the one you have been praying about for so long."

"My main question to God is why, not how."

The trail veered off to the north again and up a steep incline. As they approached level ground Ben took a seat on a rock. "Is it okay to stop for a bit to catch my breath?" he asked, not waiting for permission.

"Certainly. Our destination is not as important as our

journey in this case. So you believe that your main question is 'Why did God allow Jake to get Alzheimer's?'"

"Yes. *Why*."

"What kind of answer are you looking for?"

"The truth. That's all."

"And you believe that getting the answer to your why question will allow you to better cope with Jake's condition?"

"It seems logical to me."

"I am not questioning your logic, but I am concerned that your quest for the ultimate answer to this why question might not be the end to your questions regarding this matter."

"So you can't tell me why?" Ben paused for a few seconds and wondered if he was a bit too disrespectful with his last question. *After all, this is no human being I'm talking with*, he thought. He continued. "I mean, is this one of those 'off limits' questions?"

"Not completely, no. But the why's of the universe often remain hidden to all created beings, including me. Perhaps you are jumping to the why question too quickly."

"What do you mean?"

Apokrin took a seat on a large fallen tree on the opposite side of the trail and faced Ben. "Throughout history, and especially as outlined in the Bible, people have started with the why question. But your kind can not really completely comprehend the answer. You are created in His image, but you are also limited, finite."

"So we're not supposed to ask why?"

"I did not say you could not ask."

"What's the good of asking if you won't get an answer?"

"It is not that God will not answer. I am here, am I

not? How familiar are you with the Son's Sermon on the Mount?"

"I know most of it I think."

"Do you remember His words about asking for bread and receiving a stone?"

"Yeah. Jesus said that if we ask God for bread He won't give us a stone because He loves us."

"And implicit in His words is the idea that if you are truly seeking God, He will not give you something that is bad for you even if it looks like it is good for you."

"Yeah, I suppose."

"Asking the why question too quickly is much like asking for a stone. The answer could do you more harm then good, and God knows that. Your how question is better at this time."

"My how question?"

"How do you have a relationship with someone if you can not communicate with them."

"So that's a good one, eh?"

"Very good."

"What's the answer?"

"Ah. That is simple. You can not."

"So you're telling me I'm supposed to just be resolved to the unpleasant fact that my relationship with Jake is just over? We're supposed to just grin and bear it and wait for him to die?"

"No. I am not telling you that."

"So what are you telling me?"

"That you can not have a relationship with someone you can not communicate with."

"That's not really rocket science."

"No, but do not be so sure that you know what communication is."

"So I can communicate with Jake even now, in his condition?"

"Yes."

chapter 7

David headed toward the breakfast lounge hoping the cappuccino machine was working this late at night. He never was much for coffee, but he kind of liked the extra milk and sugar that cappuccino offered.

"Bingo!" he said out loud as his Styrofoam cup started to fill. *If I can't sleep at least I might as well relax down here for a while*, he thought. He grabbed the sports page out of a *USA Today* and sat down to sip and read.

After re-reading the same paragraph four times and still having no clue what it said, he started thinking again about this weekend, his grandpa, and his dad. He always thought Grandpa Jake was too strong for something like Alzheimer's. He began drifting into a familiar prayer. *Why God? Wouldn't it be better if he would have just died of a heart attack or something?* A few moments later he was startled as his paper was ripped out of his hands. He looked up to see. "Mom! What are you doing down here?"

"That's what I was going to ask you."

"I just couldn't sleep, so I thought I'd come down here and read."

"And drink this hyper-caffeine too? That should help your sleeping problems a lot!" She grinned and poured herself a cup before joining him at the table.

"I've been awake for the past hour or so too. But I didn't think I'd see you down here." She grabbed him by the hand. "David, you never have trouble sleeping. You okay?"

"Oh, yeah. I'm fine. Just a lot to think about I guess."

"There's nothing wrong with going to a community college for a year or two before entering the university. Besides it's cheaper and you get to live at home for a while longer."

"Oh that. Yeah, that's probably what I'll do."

"So that's not what was keeping you up?"

"Well, no, not really. I've just been thinking a lot lately about deeper stuff, you know. Like what's going on with Grandpa—and Dad." His voiced trailed off at the end, almost like he wished he would have kept the conversation to something safer like college.

chapter 8

Ben set silent for a moment on the rock, wondering if he had heard Apokrin wrong. "Did you just say yes to my last question?"

"You heard me correctly."

"So there *is* a way to communicate with Jake? How? He can hardly put two words together when he does talk. His mind seems…gone."

"Things are not always as they seem. There are many ways to communicate—even for humans."

"Humans—are you saying that you can communicate in ways we can't?"

"Yes."

"How? In what ways?"

"I am afraid that going down the trail this conversation may lead to could be frustrating for you."

"Frustrating? Why?"

"You are fallen man, personally redeemed, but, very mortal. I am not fallen, and I am not man. There are things I understand that you simply cannot."

"So we're back to square one again? I ask questions and you say you can't answer them?"

Apokrin stood and faced Ben before he spoke again. His eyes were gleaming as Ben looked up and into them. Ben felt a mixture of excitement, longing, and fear. Finally, Apokrin spoke, "Do you really think we are merely at square one? Have you learned nothing from my visit and our conversation?"

Ben could not tell if Apokrin was angry or simply direct, but his tone had changed from the soothing calmness Ben had apparently taken for granted. "I'm sorry for what I said. No, I don't believe we are still at square one. I have enjoyed our hike and conversation very much. You have been so easy to talk to I just kind of forgot who you really are."

Apokrin smiled and put out his large hand to help Ben up. "Apology accepted. I am glad you have been able to be comfortable around me. But do not forget who I am. I am not human. I am created but not mortal…and…I would not want to have to kill you."

Ben stiffened up and shrunk back a bit. Then Apokrin burst out laughing. "That was a joke. I am sorry if I frightened you."

Ben let out a huge breath and set back down and wiped his forehead. "Whew. Well it's not like it would be all that hard for you. My mind was racing there for a second. I thought back to the Bible passages where angels were used for such things."

"Yes, but that was very much the exception, not the rule. And only when He willed it, and never in any arbitrary fashion."

"But sometimes it seems very arbitrary, like, not all of the people seemed so wicked."

"Things are not always as they seem. Man's view is very limited. Does the God of the Bible seem to be a blood-thirsty, power-hungry killer?"

"Well no. Not usually."

"But sometimes?"

"Well a few times in the Old Testament, it looks like God jumps to judgment too quickly, like in Joshua when whole towns are wiped out, kids and all."

"There were warnings, calls to repentance, grace given but not received."

"But the Bible doesn't always talk about those warnings and that grace."

"The Bible is written by His power but through the agents of His choice. Their perspective is all they could write from."

"So you're saying that those times when it looks like God is being all about judgment that there really was grace given, but the biblical writer simply wasn't aware of it?"

"Yes. Something like that. Can I ask you a question?"

Ben nodded.

"How do you best know what the character of God is?"

"From the Bible."

"Yes. And what did I already say is central to this?"

"Well…Jesus."

"Correct. The Son clearly shows God's character because He is God. Now from what you know of Him, would He give people pure judgment and no grace?"

"No He wouldn't. He is all about grace."

"*Never forget*, Ben, God in the book of Joshua is the Son. The Son is not all of God but He is fully God and His character will not deviate from one century to the next. His servant John wrote well about this in His Gospel."

"I guess I kind of forgot about that."

"Many Christians do, to their detriment. I know it is hard to comprehend, God as Father, Son, and Holy Spirit always existing and never created. It is even beyond my comprehension. But it is the truth."

"So angels don't know everything then?"

"No, far from it. We are not human, but we are created beings."

"But so many people think that angels used to be people on earth. Like Clarence in *It's a Wonderful Life*."

"That movie is a great movie to help people see that they have purpose in their lives, but not so good on angelology."

"Angelology?"

"Yes, the study and doctrine of angels. The Bible gives glimpses of what we are like but does not give systematic information regarding our nature, abilities, and origin. You are given sufficient information for what you need, however, we are almost always described by what we do, not who we are."

"I've read a few books on angels. Some of them go into a lot of detail."

"I assume they are well-meaning, but one should not go further than the text allows. We are not the focal point of the book. We are merely messengers and agents of God. Infatuation with us can cause much harm and can cause people to miss the truth of the gospel. I have seen it in many time periods."

"So books on angels are bad for us?"

"Not all of them. Those that do not add to what is revealed in the Bible can be beneficial. However, many such books have taken what is not known and left hidden and brought it into the 'known' by mere extrapolation and conjecture. God saw to it that you have what you need in His Word. Adding to it, or varying from it, will only cause problems. But before we get any deeper into this, let us start walking again."

Apokrin helped Ben up again and they began climbing the trail toward the peak as the sky started to show a hint of brightening.

chapter 9

"I knew that Grandpa's illness bothered you, but I didn't know it was bothering you this much," Barb said after a long pause.

"Doesn't it bother all of us Mom? I mean we all believe in Jesus and try to follow Him, but I have no clue why something like this would happen to Grandpa Jake and I don't think any of us know why, even Aunt Claire."

"I suppose you're right. We all struggle with it in our own way but we don't really say much about that part of it...the why question I mean."

"We never talk about it. It's like we're being unfaithful if we ask the question. But how do we just accept something like this. Grandpa was always someone I looked up to. But now...well, it's just hard to see him that way."

Barb started to speak but no sound came out. To hear her oldest son express the same struggles she had was both comforting and heart-breaking. Despite her best efforts, the tears started to flow.

"I'm sorry Mom," David said as he leaned over and patted her shoulder. "It must be even harder for you, I mean, he's your dad. You've known him a lot longer than I have."

Barb broke a long moment of silence as she wiped the tears away from her eyes with the sleeve of her robe. "You're right David. We do need to talk about this more. Dad and I have tried to a few times…it's just so hard…to know where to start. Do you know what I mean?"

"Well let's just start somewhere…anywhere…the Bible, information about Alzheimer's, just everyone talking about where they are with the whole thing. And we should include the younger kids, too. Nat is struggling too, I can tell. Heck, it seems like Liz is handling it better than the rest of us."

"Lizzy? But she's only ten?"

"I know, but I heard Nat and her talking about going to see Grandpa one day. Nat didn't want to go but Liz kept coaxing her. Finally Nat yelled, 'He's not going to know we're there anyway!' Liz just said back, "Oh, yes he will, I know he will. God takes care of that.'"

"Oh to be that young and not understand."

"Maybe she understands better than the rest of us. Maybe it's not misunderstanding, but just…faith."

chapter 10

As they approached a part of the trail lined with dense spruce trees, Ben started the conversation again. "So you were created, but you're not human."

"That is correct. I am not fallen like you, or mortal. I never was and I never will be."

"Do you remember when you were created?"

"Not completely, but soon after. Like it was yesterday."

"But wasn't it a long time ago?"

"Yes it was. But time is something you are a slave to and I am not."

"So you aren't bound by time?"

"I did not say that. I said I was not a slave to it. Only He is not time bound, except when He chose to be. But I am afraid I must frustrate you again. There is really no way we can have this conversation at this time. I would not be able to explain the time concept to you, and you would not be able to comprehend it. It would not be beneficial and would only serve to confuse. But, I can offer you one example…a bit of a glimpse into the difference between what time means to you and what it means to Him. Would you like that?"

"Certainly."

"Do you remember what contributed to my coming to you?"

"God wanted you to answer some of my questions."

"Yes. But what was it I told you aided God's desire?"

"My prayers?"

"Yes, and the prayers of many others."

"What does that have to do with the time question?"

"How many people do you think prayed to God in the last…week?"

"Millions, maybe billions."

"And yet God heard your prayer and the prayers of your family along with those billions of other prayers. He has revealed that He hears all prayers a number of times in His word. Have you ever thought of how He does this?"

"Well, no. Not really. Not until now I guess." Ben stopped on the trail for a moment as the thought moved through his mind. He caught up to Apokrin and asked, "So how does it work?"

"I can not tell you exactly how it works, but I do know it has much to do with God not being time bound. He has 'all the time in the world' as you might say. Or better put, the universe. And not only does He hear each prayer uttered, He deals with each one, 'spends time' with it you might say; they are all important to Him. His word is true."

"I really never thought of it that way. I always believed that God heard our prayers, but never really thought about how He could do that."

"The temptation to think about your own problems and your own self is a great one. It is easy to forget about those around you. But, in some ways, when you pray, it is just you and God. He has made it that way."

Apokrin stopped and put his hand on Ben's shoulder. He pointed up to the peak of the mountain, now much closer than before, and said, "Our journey ends at that peak. I know you have many questions, but we must get back to dealing with the main questions that you have that I came to address."

Ben looked at the peak no more than an hour away. He felt bad that he had probed into these other questions and had left so little time to talk about dealing with Jake's condition. He turned and looked straight at Apokrin. "Why does Jake have Alzheimer's?"

chapter 11

Barb sipped her cappuccino for a moment and then quietly said one word, "Faith."

"Yeah Mom, I really think Liz just has faith."

"Oh, I don't doubt that she does. But I think that's the reason all of us dodge talking about Grandpa. At least it is for me…I think."

"You think that if we question Grandpa's illness it shows a lack of faith?"

"No. No, that's not what I mean. I think if I question his illness truthfully, it may cause me to conclude that my questions have no real answers. I guess I'm just scared that asking questions about my dad having Alzheimer's will end up making me question everything about my faith."

"Do you think if we were faithful enough, God would heal Grandpa?"

"Sometimes I do think that. I certainly don't think that healing him would be a problem for God's power. But that verse from Hebrews chapter eleven keeps coming back to me: 'Faith…is being…certain of what we do not see.'" She looked up at David and repeated slowly, "Of what we do not see."

"Do not see?"

"Faith apparently is not all about seeing things, miraculous things, successful things. But Jesus certainly did a lot of miraculous things while He was on earth, didn't he?"

"Pastor Jeff just talked about that in youth group last week. He said people did seem to believe in Jesus after His miracles, but that when He quit doing them the last week of His life, most people left Him and thought He was a fake."

"So are we saying that if Jesus doesn't heal Grandpa now that He is a fake? Maybe I don't understand what faith really is."

David yawned, "Me either. Not completely anyway."

"We better get back to the room and get some sleep. Do you think we should try to make it to the cabin tomorrow?"

"Yeah. I do"

"Me too."

"So, straight to the why question again," Apokrin replied as he again started walking up the path. "I thought you understood that we can not start there."

"But we don't have much time now."

"True. But we were going down the right path there for a while."

"We were?"

"Yes, when we were talking about not being able to have a relationship with someone you can not communicate with. We started delving in to the issue of what true communication really is."

"Yeah, now I remember. You said that there were ways of

communication that weren't verbal. So does Jake know I'm there when I come to see him?"

"In one way or another he does."

"So he can still hear me, feel my touch, understand me?"

"Perhaps in some ways, but not the way you might think."

"What do you mean?"

"I said that Jake has knowledge of your presence when you are there. How much knowledge, and how deep it is, I do not know."

"But you assure me that he does in some ways 'know?'"

"Yes."

"So our visits do matter to him," Ben muttered to himself. "How does he know this? How do we communicate with him?"

"Your voice, your touch, and even your smell may help. But communication with someone in Jake's condition is mainly by your presence and your prayers."

"My prayers?"

chapter 12

"Dad and I have talked about this stuff a little bit," David began again after a long pause where both of them came close to dozing off.

"You did? When?"

"When I rode home with him after my last football game, it came up." David got up and threw his coffee cup into the trash and slowly stretched his arms above his head looking very tired.

"Well?"

"Well, what?"

"What did you guys talk about? I've tried to talk to him a number of times but he always finds a way to avoid it."

"I guess he couldn't avoid it as much in the car, but he still did a good job of changing the subject, usually to sports."

"But did he ever really talk about it?"

"The only thing he really said that wasn't just small talk was something about needing some time to process the whole ordeal, but he didn't get very specific."

Barb got up and threw her cup away too. "Maybe all of us need to have a family meeting when we get to the cabin.

For now let's go get at least a bit of sleep before we venture up that mountain."

David yawned and nodded in agreement.

The sky was beginning to fill with stars as Ben and Apokrin came out of the pine trees and into another clearing. "How do my prayers communicate with Jake?" Ben continued.

"What is prayer, Ben?"

"Talking with God."

"Communicating?"

"Yeah, I guess you could call it that. But I don't think I've ever really been communicated back to."

"So you have never heard God's voice?"

"No, not really, not audibly. I guess a few times it seems like I've received some direction. It's hard to be certain. Nothing like what happened in biblical times, that's for sure."

"That was a different time."

"So you're saying that God works differently now?"

"For the most part, yes."

"Why?"

"Let me ask you a question." Apokrin glanced at the mountain peak that was very close now and stopped walking. He turned to Ben. "You said it seemed like you got some direction from God in your communication with Him. How did you know it was from Him?"

"I don't know. I guess it just sounded like something He would tell me, and it wasn't necessarily what I thought was best."

"Sounded like something He would tell you? How did you know that?"

"It kind of sounded like directions God might give someone in the Bible."

"So it seemed in character for God?"

"Yeah, it matched up with the God of the Bible."

"There is no other." Apokrin began walking toward the peak again. "Why do you think God would normally work differently now than in the time of the Bible?"

"I don't know. I guess we have more information now."

"*Yes!* That is wisdom. And not just any information. You have the entire Biblical revelation; they did not."

"So that's why God doesn't appear in burning bushes and talk directly to prophets anymore?"

"I did not say He does not, or even that He will not, but that the Word has been given. It is now primary. Any human who does not seek to know and understand it does so to their own peril."

"So the Bible is the center of Christianity now?"

"The Son is always the center. But the Bible is God's revelation and points to that fact."

"I guess that does make sense. If God went to the trouble to reveal all of this important info to us, the least we could do is try to know it and study it."

"Well said. The Bible is the standard humans must use. For instance, how do you know I am from God?"

Ben stopped and sat down on the incline on the west side of the path. His heart sank a bit and fear crept in. The idea that Apokrin was anything other than what he said he was had never occurred to him. He looked up to see the angel looking directly into his eyes. He looked away, not knowing what to think. His mind raced until he quickly realized what he really could count on. The fear left him and assurance came into his heart. He stood. "I am no Bible scholar, but everything you have told me lines up with it, you have said nothing that contradicts it."

"Good. Good. And I will not."

chapter 13

Barb and David slowly opened the hotel room door and crept back in; Barb to the bed beside Natalie and David back to his pillow and blanket on the floor. The clock read 3:47 a.m. *Hopefully we can get a good four hours in before we have to get up again*, Barb thought as she slipped under the covers next to Natalie.

She was almost asleep when she heard Natalie whisper, "Mom."

"What?" Barb whispered back.

"Where were you?"

"David and I were just talking and we didn't want to wake you guys up."

"What were you talking about?"

"Don't worry about that right now, honey. Let's get some sleep. We'll talk about it in the morning." Barb rolled over and closed her eyes.

"It was about Grandpa wasn't it," Natalie whispered back.

"Yes."

"I want to pray for him, but I don't know what to say that hasn't already been said."

"Just tell God what's on your heart."

"But He already knows."

"But He tells us to be persistent, so just keep trying."

Natalie yawned an "Okay, Mom." and quietly whispered "night."

Barb thought, *"Just keep trying." I think I need to take my own advice.*

The cloud cover had almost lifted and countless stars lit up the cool night sky as Ben and his hiking partner took a break on a large rock very near the peak. "I love it up here," Ben said as he broke the silence. "It's so peaceful. Untouched."

"It is very beautiful," Apokrin replied.

"Nothing like heaven I bet." Ben continued to stare at the star lit sky as he tried to imagine what heaven might be like.

"This is a glimpse."

"Of heaven?"

"Yes. But just a very small glimpse."

"Jake used to love to just come up to the peak and sit and look at the sky. At sunrise, sunset, and any time in between. But he can't do that now."

"I suppose not completely."

"What do you mean, *not completely*?"

"Simply that I agree with you that he probably would not enjoy it as much as he used to if you brought him up here now."

"As much? How 'bout, not at all! He can't even remember who we are, how would he even know he was up here?"

"Knowing that how may go a long way in answering your main prayer."

"My main prayer?"

"Yes. Your petition to 'help me make sense out of all of this stuff Jake is going through.'"

"So he would know that he was up here?"

"In some ways he would."

"What ways?"

"Memories and the Spirit."

"Memories? He can't remember anything!"

Apokrin shifted his weight and turned to look directly at Ben. Ben was again somewhat mesmerized by his eyes. So deep, so compassionate, so wise, so meaningful. "Ben. What I am going to tell you now will have to be understood primarily on faith. Do you know the last line written in the Gospel that the apostle Matthew wrote?"

Ben thought a moment. He and Barb had gone through a Bible study on Matthew with a few other couples. "The last line," Ben mumbled to himself. Finally he blurted out, "The Great Commission!" feeling a bit proud of himself.

"Yes, Matthew did end with that, but the very last sentence that he records is from the lips of the Son. 'And be sure of this: I am with you always, even to the end of the age.'"

Ben started to reply but then sat quietly in thought.

"Ben, focus on the promise of the Son. 'I am with you always.'"

Ben repeated those words over and over in his mind. He

finally looked up at Apokrin and it hit him. "So He is with me even when you aren't here to answer my questions."

Apokrin let out a little sigh. "Yes, Ben, He is, but I was not talking about you, I was thinking of Jake."

chapter 14

Almost 200 miles away from Mystery Peak, Claire woke up a bit startled. She soon recognized that she was facing the window in her dad's room at the nursing home. She turned around to see Jake curled up and sound asleep. She got up out of the chair and moved toward the window. Kneeling down, she folded her hands and bowed her head.

"Heavenly Father, I'm not sure why I woke up, but I do know that you are listening to my prayer right now. I truly feel that you have prompted me to offer this prayer to you. You have placed Ben on my heart, to pray for him, for his understanding, for his faith. Help him understand what you are trying to tell him. And continue to be with Dad, and our whole family. In Jesus name, Amen."

"Jake? But he can't even communicate with his own family. How could he know that God is with him?"

"Ben, do not look at everything from an earthly perspective. That promise you have been meditating on, do you think it is just for people who can communicate in what you see as a normal way?"

Ben looked and felt a bit confused. A few times he started to speak, but wasn't quite sure what to say. And then his heart, his entire chest, started to feel warm. Goose pimples ran over his entire body. A feeling, but something more than that, an assurance filled his heart and mind.

"Jesus is with Jake?!"

"That promise is never more true than at this time in someone's life."

Ben paused a moment. "But how does it work?"

Apokrin stood up and smiled. Ben waited, but the angel didn't speak. Ben finally broke the silence, "Is this one of those off limits questions?"

Apokrin walked a little way back down the path and then back to Ben, then turned again, almost pacing. "It is not that it is off limits, Ben. I want to word this in such a way that you will understand it best."

Ben tried to be patient as he waited for Apokrin to speak. After a few minutes he finally did. "When someone is in Jake's condition, one where normal communication with others is very limited or ceases altogether, God is with them in a special way."

Ben tried to reply but the angel put his hand up toward Ben's mouth and said quietly, "Not now. Just listen. There is comfort and peace given in a greater measure than before; fear is removed and peace is received. In your normal life, Ben, you have all of your senses. That is a blessing, but it can be a distraction. It can be harder to discern important things, and harder to listen.

"Someone who has Alzheimer's, dementia, or a stroke that limits their ability to communicate with the outside world has a special place in God's heart, and He does not sit idly by, waiting for their death. He acts in a real way, coming to them in ways you can only partially imagine. 'Blessed are the poor in spirit, for theirs is the kingdom of heaven.' This is but one way that this blessing is fulfilled, to those who are lacking in ability, God comes to their aid. The world may not know it, but it is true."

Apokrin stopped speaking and sat down opposite of the trail from Ben, but Ben remained quiet, hoping and longing for more. The angel's words were so crisp and real, so refreshing, like something he always wondered about but yet somehow already knew.

Apokrin sighed and quietly continued, "The visits you and others have made to Jake are often known by him. In some way and in some time: God's way and God's time. Jake, and others like him do not necessarily have a physical perception of someone's presence or words, but with God's help, they are communicated to in non-verbal ways. There is 'soul communication' that goes beyond mere words—comfort given, peace received."

Ben's mind was racing, along with his heart. He was trying to comprehend what he was hearing, trying to remember every precious word. The two sat in silence for a long while.

Suddenly Apokrin broke the silence, "My time with you is coming to an end." He stood up and put out his hand for Ben to grab it. "Come, let us finish this journey."

Ben took his huge hand and stood up. He then followed the angel toward the peak of the mountain only a few hundred yards away.

chapter 15

Barb rolled over and pressed the snooze button for the third time. *It can't be morning already*, she thought. As she opened her eyes she saw mostly darkness—and then Greg's wide, toothless grin.

"Tricked you, Mom!"

Barb let her head gravitate back to the pillow mumbling, "How did you trick me, Greg?"

"There's still time to watch the sunrise!"

Sunrise? Barb thought. *What time is it?* She rolled over and looked at the alarm clock. 6:47 a.m.

"Greg. What time did you set this for?"

"6:28 a.m. That way you have time to get woke up to watch the sunrise with me."

Barb tried to clear her head and figure out what in the world Greg was talking about. Then she remembered. Her dad always said that the most beautiful sunrises were at the foot of the mountains after a snow. He must have passed this information on to Greg.

"Come on Mom, we'll miss it. It's in ten minutes and we

can see it great out of our window," Greg said as he tugged on Barb's arm.

"Okay, okay, honey. I'm getting up." She rolled out of bed and headed to the bathroom to splash water in her face. Both Liz and Natalie were already up. David was lying on the floor with a pillow over his head. After brushing her teeth, gargling, and drying her face, Barb walked over to the hotel window that faced directly east.

"T-w-o-o-o min-ut-es!" Greg informed them all in an NBA announcer type voice.

As the seconds passed by, David stood up and sleepily peered over Greg to look outside too. The five of them were all staring at the base of the mountain when the first light showed itself. The light danced off the snow and the ice crystal covered trees showing a brilliance and level of color that dazzled them all. None of them spoke—they just soaked it in.

Finally, Barb broke the silence with a quiet whisper, "Dad was right."

As Apokrin and Ben neared the peak for the first time, Ben started looking around at his surroundings. He had been so involved in thought and the conversation that he completely lost track of time. As he looked off to the east, he stopped to watch the first glimpse of light come over the horizon.

Apokrin stood now too, watching with those deep eyes, a slight smile on his face.

For the next few minutes both of them stood motionless and silent as the sun lit up the mountain. At first the colors were dim, but as the light grew the colors seemed to jump out second by second. The two beings enjoyed this sunrise never saying a word, but somehow communicating, understanding and appreciating the wonder and power of the God that created both of them.

chapter 16

David threw the last bag on the heap in the back of the SUV and slammed the doors shut. "Come on, Nat, you know you'll have fun once we get up there," he said to his younger sister who was the lone dissenter.

"I know," she said as she fumbled with her iPod, "but I thought all of this snow would send us back home and I could still make it to Sheila's party."

"Why would you want to hang around a bunch of goofy girls when you could spend time with your wonderful family?"

"It's just that Sheila just turned sixteen—it's a special birthday."

David looked at his watch, "What's taking Mom so long? Anyway, Sheila's the dingiest one of the bunch."

"Oh be quiet," Natalie shot back. "You know she has a crush on you don't you?"

"Yeah, since like the third grade."

"David's got a girlfriend! David's got a girlfriend!" Greg chanted from the back seat.

"The luggage rack is still empty, Greg, and I've got a couple of bungee cords that would keep you secure, so shut up."

Greg withdrew back into the SUV, not sure if his older, and much bigger, brother was kidding or not.

Barb came jogging out of the front door of the hotel and threw the keys to David. "Okay, your turn," she said as she opened the passenger-side door.

"What took so long?" David asked as he jumped into the driver's seat and put on his seat belt.

"I had a discussion with the hotel manager about the broken pool."

"You didn't ask for a reduced rate did you Mom?"

"I sure did, and got it. The sign says pool, not broken pool."

David rolled his eyes, started the SUV, and began heading for the highway.

Just then a small voice came from the back seat. "I gotta go to the bathroom."

Barb and Natalie yelled simultaneously, "*Greg!*"

"Hey, better now than later," David said as he pulled back around to the front of the hotel. "And, squirt, hurry up, those bungee cords might just come in handy yet."

Greg jumped out of the car and sprinted back into the hotel door.

chapter 17

As the full sun came into view, Apokrin began walking again. Ben didn't walk beside him like he had for most of the journey, but a bit behind him. Ben wanted to continue their conversation, but wasn't sure if it was appropriate at this time. As they came around a small pine tree they both saw the very peak of the mountain. Their journey to Mystery Peak was over.

Apokrin walked to the apex of the mountain and put his hands in the air and took in a deep breath. "The beauty of creation. It is magnificent," he said, gazing at the scenery. "What an awesome God we worship."

"Worship? You worship God too?"

"Certainly. It is a privilege to praise the one true God. Always."

"Sometimes my mind wanders in worship. I don't always get a lot out of worship services."

"Remember what worship is for: to praise God, to listen to Him, to come close to your very reason for existence. Often you will only get out what you put in to it."

"But I know some pretty good guys that don't attend worship all that often."

Apokrin shook his head. "That is a great disappointment to God. I do not understand how someone who says they follow the Son could neglect coming to worship Him with those who proclaim the same allegiance. There is no such Christianity in the Bible. It is assumed that believers in the Son will worship together to show their commitment, to seek Him, to serve Him, to show that they really do love Him."

"But some worship services are more inspiring than others. They make you feel better."

"Perhaps. But *feeling good* is not the purpose of worship. It is to experience God and give yourself anew to Him. To thank Him, to get closer to Him. It is a mystery, even to me, how worship really works. But it is a gift to humanity, and neglecting it is foolish. Do not take the mystery out of worship—let God be God and trust Him."

"Understanding is a wonderful blessing, Ben, but it is not everything. Some things must be taken on faith. Take the Bible's word for it: 'do not give up meeting together to worship the one true God.'"

Apokrin paused a moment to allow Ben to respond, but Ben was still trying to process what he had just heard. "Our time together must now end, Ben."

Ben slowly walked over to him and looked into his eyes again. Apokrin sensed the sudden sorrow in Ben. "Why so sad? Has our time together not been fruitful?"

"Oh no. That's not it. I have learned more about my life in this one night than all of the others put together."

"That is probably an exaggeration," Apokrin mused as he put his hand on Ben's shoulder. "But I am glad that your prayers have been answered. Or have they?"

Ben looked away for a moment, not knowing if he should say what he was thinking or not.

Apokrin's voice brought him back. "What is it? Does the why question still trouble you?"

"You said I can't ask the why question."

"I did not say you could not ask it, just that you should not start with it."

"So it is okay to ask now?"

"Do you still feel it is necessary?"

"That's the problem. I don't know what I think about it now. With Jake so securely in God's hands, should why even matter anymore?"

"That is a question you will have to answer for yourself."

Ben struggled with his thoughts and then decided that he may never get another chance to ask the question, so he quietly asked, "Why did Jake get Alzheimer's?"

"I do not think you will like my answer."

Ben waited patiently saying nothing.

"I am sorry, Ben, but I do not know."

Apokrin put his hand up continuing, "But before you question that answer, let me complete it. I am not God, simply His servant. I am not all powerful, nor do I have all knowledge. As to the specifics of why Jake got this disease, I do not know. But I do know that God's promises are true, and by now you should know that too."

"God's written word shows you clearly what He is like, and His promise to be with Jake and never leave him is one that you can be assured of. All I can tell you is what the Father told me once when I desired to know the why of a given situation."

Apokrin paused; making sure that Ben was listening attentively, "He said, 'That knowledge is not for you at this time. Trust me.' So I do."

"But that isn't enough for some people."

"That is true. But is it enough for you?"

Ben thought for a moment, about Jake in his nursing home bed, about all of his prayers to God about Jake's condition, and about his prayers for Jake's healing. "But Apokrin, I prayed for God to heal him, to take the disease away, to reverse its affects."

"Do you believe God answered your prayer?"

"It doesn't look like it."

"Do you think He heard it?"

"Yes. Yes, I do think He heard it."

"Then it was answered."

"But Jake is still sick."

"Yes he is. Ben, you must understand by now, from our conversation regarding communicating at least, that what you see as healing and what God sees as healing is not always going to be the same. Do you believe that God knows what is best for Jake?"

"Yeah."

"Even better than you do?"

"Certainly."

"Then just trust Him Ben and understand this..." Apokrin paused and slowly looked around at the view from the mountaintop. Ben peered back at him, waiting for his next comment. "The healing miracles of the Son were used primarily to show who He was and to fulfill what was prophesied regarding the Messiah. They were never meant to be the focal point of His ministry. They were never meant to be worshipped. God heard your prayer and has answered it. In every life, at some point in time, the answer to the prayer for bodily healing will be…no."

"No?"

"If it is from God, you must trust Him." Apokrin placed his other hand on Jake's shoulder and looked down at him. "I have enjoyed our time together, friend, but my assignment here is over. I must go."

Ben looked up at those deep, penetrating yet compassionate eyes, as a tear fell from one of his. "Thank you."

"You are welcome," Apokrin said as he stepped away from Ben.

"Wait! Will I ever see you again?" Ben shouted as Apokrin quickly walked away from him.

"Not in this life, friend," the angel replied as he glanced back and gave a wave.

"Any last words?!" Ben yelled back as loud as he could.

"Hebrews 13:5," Apokrin said as he walked toward the edge of the cliff. And just as quickly as he had appeared, he was gone.

chapter 18

Ben stood on the peak of the mountain for a long while thinking, wondering, *So was this all real?* He recalled Apokrin's words while they were still in the cabin, "There will always be the temptation to question its reality."

"Well it looks like that's started already." Ben took another look around. The sun was climbing through a few thin clouds on the horizon as he decided to make the long hike back to the cabin. "The way back down will sure be easier, but a whole lot more boring…and lonely."

He had walked only a few yards when he saw something dark on the other side of the pine trees. There were very few bears around this part of the mountains anymore, but he didn't want to meet one of them unarmed and with his back toward the peak. He quietly moved toward a small pine tree and ducked down behind it, whispering a prayer, "Lord protect me up here. I can't believe you would bless me with this visit and then have me mauled by a bear."

As Ben's pulse and heart quickened the animal shot out from behind the trees and landed on him. He let out a fearful yell and turned to struggle away from its grip. As he opened his eyes he focused on a large black nose around dark brown fur and suddenly felt a large, wet tongue licking his face. "Gabe! You scared the heck out of me, boy! I was so focused on our heavenly messenger that I hardly noticed you following us." Gabe continued to lick Ben's face and vigorously wag his tail.

"Well I guess the trip back down won't be as lonely as I thought." Ben rubbed the dog's head behind the ears. "Come on boy. Let's head back."

———————————————

As David drove up the thin and winding mountain road he was careful to stay far to the right when going around a curve. There was really no way of knowing if someone was coming the other way since most of the turns were blind and a half a dozen reminders from Barb instilled a bit of extra caution in him. He was anxious to see and talk with his dad about all of the stuff he had been thinking and feeling the past couple of days, along with Aunt Claire's phone call. *And now even Mom*, David thought as he came to the one-mile marker, a huge pine tree that split the road in two for about a hundred yards.

"One mile left!" Greg yelled from the back seat.

A few minutes later the SUV pulled up next to the old pickup on the north side of the cabin. David went to the back of the car to start bringing in the luggage while the other four headed for the cabin. Before Barb could get into the front door it slammed open as Greg appeared. "Dad's not here."

"He's probably fishing at the creek," Barb replied as she walked into the cabin. She walked through the cabin's front room and into the kitchen. *No dirty dishes, that's a surprise,* she thought as she glanced into the sink.

"A little help please!" David yelled as he stumbled through the front door carrying five bags.

Barb ran over and grabbed two of them, "Where are the other three kids?"

"Looking for Dad I guess," David said as he took the remaining bags off his shoulders and headed back outside.

Barb took the two bags into the bedroom and set them on the bed. She turned to walk out of the room, but paused and looked back. She noticed that the bed spread was hanging down about an inch from the floor, not tucked under the mattress like Ben always did it. *I wonder why he didn't sleep in the bed last night,* she thought.

chapter 19

Gabe turned and ran back toward Ben as he took yet another rest on a tree stump by the path. "I thought going down would be easier, but I guess the lack of sleep has caught up with me boy," he rubbed Gabe's head and glanced toward the east.

The time that he had spent with Apokrin had gone so fast. It seemed like minutes, but it had ended up being almost ten hours. Sleep had not entered his mind during their conversation, but caught up to him now. He went another half-mile down the trail, struggling to make it back to the cabin. A nice flat, inviting boulder offered him a new resting place, and he took it. The rock was large enough to lie on and even offered a sort of pillow for his head. Within a few minutes, Ben had drifted off to sleep.

"Well, I'm going hiking," David said as he got up from the couch to put on his shoes.

"Me too," Greg added as he ran in from the kitchen.

"It's almost lunch time," Barb replied. "I think it would be best if we just waited for Dad here."

"It's 11:15," David said as he glanced at his watch. "We'll just go up the trail for thirty minutes and then head back. That way we'll be back in an hour and in time for lunch."

Barb started to disagree, but she was thinking of the same thing and she knew that David would look after Greg well. "Okay," she relented.

As the two boys headed past the cars down the road, David asked his little brother, "Which trail should we try?"

"Dad's favorite of course," Greg replied.

"Off to Mystery Peak it is."

They went another hundred yards and then darted into the trees to catch the main trail. Within a few minutes they were headed up the mountain toward the peak. Greg broke the silence, "David?"

"Yeah."

"Do you think Dad's okay?"

"Why would you ask that?"

"I dunno. It's just not like him to break the 'number one hiking rule.'"

"The buddy rule?"

"Well if he did hike to the peak, he would have had to do it on his own. He always tells us to never hike alone. It just seems weird that he would do it."

David continued to keep a quick pace up the trail, trying to get the most distance out of thirty minutes he could. But he knew Greg was right, it didn't make sense. "Maybe he found a friend to hike with," David said, trying to pacify Greg and change the subject.

Jake awoke from a deep sleep and stared blankly at the ceiling of his room. The room was dimly lit and the curtain was drawn. Aside from the pictures his daughters had placed on the wall and the cribbage board on his nightstand, the room looked quite institutional. An aid came in and opened the curtains. "How about a little sunshine in this room?" she said as she pulled the curtains open and turned back to Jake. "You remember your favorite aid, Joan, don't you, Jake?" she continued with a smile.

Joan grabbed a cup of ice and put a spoonful into Jake's mouth. He moved his mouth slowly as a portion of it trickled down his chin. Joan wiped his chin with a cloth and raised the head of the bed a bit. Jake began to make a mumbling sound.

"What's that you're trying to tell me Jake?" Joan asked as she put her ear closer to his mouth, trying to make out his words.

"N-v-er lee," Jake struggled to say.

"I'm sorry, honey, I can't quite understand you."

Jake tried again, "N-v-er lee-v"

"Never leave?" Joan asked in surprise. "Well now, Jake, I would like to stay, but I do have other patients to tend to. I'll be back in a little bit, but your daughter should be here any time. No one's going to leave you for very long."

Joan went to the bathroom to dump out the ice and came back into the room to close the curtains slightly, trying to keep the direct sun out of Jake's eyes. As she went past the bed she glanced at his face and saw the faintest of smiles on his lips. *He almost looks content right now*, she thought. *He sure looks happy about something.*

chapter 20

David glanced at his watch. He had set the chronograph timer for thirty minutes when they started up the trail and there was less than six minutes left on it. "We're going to have to turn around in about five minutes," he turned and said to Greg as he stopped to let him catch up. "Let's just go around that bend up there and take a look before we head back."

The two boys went up a sharp incline and took the path left through some bushes that had overgrown the path. As they turned back to the north they could see for a quarter of a mile up the trail to some large rocks. "Up to those rocks and then we turn around," David said as he headed toward them.

As they came closer to the rocks they both began to make out what looked like a pair of boots on one of the big flat rocks. Greg began yelling, "Dad, Dad!" hoping that the boots on the rock were attached to his dad.

Within a hundred yards they heard Gabe's familiar bark as he emerged from the rocks and ran toward them on the trail. "How you doing, boy?" Greg said as the dog knocked him to the ground and started licking his face.

David continued up the trail to meet up with his father.

As he came closer to the rock that his dad was on he noticed that the boots were not moving. A wave of fear came over him and he began sprinting to the rocks. He strode over the last part of the incline past the first few large round boulders. When his dad was almost in full view a blinding light burst into David's eyes and knocked him to the ground.

"What the heck was that?" he said out loud as he picked himself off of the trail and ran over to see if his dad was okay. At first glance David's fears were calmed as it appeared his dad was just sleeping. But as he got close enough to stand on the very rock his dad was laying on he saw it—a pool of blood under his head.

Only fifteen minutes after the boys left Barb was feeling very nervous, and so, it seemed, were Natalie and Liz. All three were sitting on the couch in the cabin quietly munching on pretzels. Liz passed the bag back to Barb and she laid it on the coffee table and let out a little laugh.

"What are you giggling about, Mom?" Natalie asked.

"Oh, I was just thinking. All these years your father and I have teased your Aunt Claire about her 'premonitions' and now I think I'm having one."

"About what?" Liz chimed in.

"I don't really know, Lizzy. I just keep getting this verse from the Psalms in my head that Grandpa used to have on his work bench. Something about angels and protection, but I can't remember the whole thing."

"I'm worried about Dad," Liz replied.

"I am too, honey, but we need to wait until the boys get

back before we start traipsing off in another direction. He's probably just fishing anyway."

After a long silence Barb asked, "Lizzy, would you go get my Bible out of my pink suitcase please. I want to see if I can find that verse."

Liz got up and disappeared into the bedroom. A few moments later she came out with her mom's Bible, searching through the concordance in the back. "The word 'angels' is in Psalm 78, 91, 103, and 148," Liz said as she walked back toward the couch.

"Look up the first one," Barb replied.

"Men ate the bread of angels; he sent them all the food they could eat."

"That's not it. Try the next one."

"He unleashed against them His hot anger, His wrath, indignation and hostility—a band of destroying angels."

"That's definitely not it!"

"Keep going."

Liz turned a few pages and began, "For He will command His angels concerning you to guard you in all your ways; they will lift you up in their hands, so that you will not strike your foot against a stone."

Liz turned to her mom and saw that her eyes were shut. *That must have been the one*, she thought as she read it to herself again. "*Guard you in all your ways.*" *Grandpa Jake could always find the coolest verses in the Bible.*

chapter 21

David composed himself and ran over to his dad, his heart racing. The pool of blood was the first thing to catch his eye. It ran onto the rock and appeared to be coming from the side of his dad's face.

David grabbed his shoulders and gently shook him, "Dad, wake up, wake up."

Immediately Ben jerked and opened his eyes trying to focus on the figure above him. *Where am I?* he thought. *And what's this goop on my face?*

After a few seconds Ben recognized David's face but still remained somewhat confused and disoriented. With David's help he struggled to sit up on the rock. Everything that had happened over the last fourteen hours raced through his mind as David attempted to wipe off the blood with his gloves.

"How long have I been asleep?" Ben mumbled, finally breaking the silence. He ran his hand along his face and followed the dried blood up to his nose. "Bloody nose…again," he said as he slowly stood up.

"Well it's 11:45 right now," David began to reply but then stopped to ask his own question.

"Dad, what were you doing out here? Are you hurt or sick?"

"It's a long story David. No. I'm not sick or hurt—just tired. I…"

Before he could get another word out Greg and Gabe came running around the corner toward them both. Greg yelled, "Dad!" and jumped on Ben.

"Be careful, Greg," David said as he began to grab Greg's arm.

"You've got blood on your face, Dad. Did you fall down?" Greg said as he felt his dad's face.

"I'm all right. Just a nose bleed. But we better start heading back to the cabin. I assume your mom and sisters are wondering where I am."

"I told Mom we would be back by a quarter after noon, so we better start back now."

As the four of them started back down the trail David said what was on his mind. "So Dad, you went hiking by yourself, violating the number one hiking rule, and then decided to take a nap on the trail?"

"I know, I know, it all looks very weird. But hopefully it will make sense if I explain the whole night. But it would probably be better to wait until we get back to the cabin to tell the whole story."

"The whole night?"

Barb jumped as the tea kettle let out a shrill whistle from the kitchen. She poured the hot water into her cup over the tea bag and then took the lunch meat and bread out of the fridge.

Natalie and Liz sorted through the bags of chips to find their favorites. As Barb went to the sink to wash off the lettuce she heard the door slam open and Gabe's familiar bark.

"Daddy!" Liz screamed as she ran across the room to give him a hug. "Where were you? We were all worried."

"Oh, just went on a little hike. But I sure am hungry."

"Well come and get it," Barb called from the kitchen.

Ben came into the kitchen and grabbed Barb and gave her a strong hug and long kiss.

"So you missed me?" Barb said, blushing a bit as the kids watched.

Ben released her and smiled at the kids, "Well let's eat!"

As the family settled down around the kitchen table Ben leaned over and whispered in Barb's ear, "I need to talk to you—right after lunch."

Barb looked at him curiously. His smile made her force a small grin herself. "Okay."

chapter 22

The family finished their lunch and began cleaning up the kitchen. "Kids. Can you guys clean up the rest of the kitchen? Mom and I have to talk about something."

"Yeah sure," David replied, glancing at Natalie.

Ben walked toward the back door and grabbed Barb's coat and his own. "So are we going on a hike?" Barb asked.

"Yeah, sort of."

"Why don't we just talk in here?"

"Hiking helps me think better, talk better."

Barb walked over and took her coat, "All right. Let's go."

Ben led the way outside the cabin door and down the road. He then turned north and picked up the Mystery Peak trail just as David and Greg had a few hours earlier. Barb began to speak a half a dozen times, but decided to remain silent until her husband began the conversation. She was extremely curious about this hike and whatever he wanted to tell her. Ben was not much of a conversationalist, which made this all the more odd. She knew there was something he had to tell her, but she had an assuring feeling that it wasn't something bad.

They had gone about a half mile when Ben led them off on a secondary trail for about fifty yards. There were three large fallen trees just off of the trail. Ben sat on the one facing north and motioned for Barb to sit on the one opposite of him so she could face him.

"I thought we were going on a hike?"

"I'm still too tired to hike very far right now. I just wanted some privacy to talk to you."

"Tired? Didn't you sleep very well last night?"

"Hardly at all."

"Ben, what's going on? What do you want to tell me?"

"I've gone over and over in my head on how to say this, but there's really no perfect way, so I'm just going to tell you."

"Tell me what?" Barb replied as she leaned forward, a concerned look on her face.

"Last night…I had a…a…visitor."

"A visitor? Someone from one of the other cabins?"

"No. This was a bit different then that."

Barb waited for him to continue, saying nothing.

"You know how I, well all of us, have been praying about Dad's condition?"

Barb nodded.

"I guess I've had just about as tough a time dealing with it as anyone. But, last night, I got a very clear answer to our prayers."

"An answer?"

"Barb. Last night I took a hike up to Mystery Peak with a messenger from God."

"You saw an angel?"

Ben hesitated, wondering what Barb was thinking—if

she would believe what he had to say. "Yes. And not only saw, but walked with, talked with, even got to know."

Barb sat there quietly feeling herself question what she just heard. But the verse from Psalm 91 came to her again. She looked into her husband's eyes. She could see the longing for a response from her. *He will command his angels concerning you*, she thought. Deep down she knew she had faith in God—right now she also knew she had to have some trust in Ben too.

"I...I believe you, honey. Please tell me what happened. I want to hear it all."

Ben stood up and grabbed her by the hand, helping her stand up. Tears were in his eyes as he gave her a long, heartfelt hug. After a few minutes they both sat down on the same tree and Ben began. "It was just a bit after ten last night. I had fallen asleep on the couch after eating a bit too much steak..."

chapter 23

David and Greg were sitting on the couch, engulfed in an assortment of fishing poles and fishing wire.

"You guys still working on those?" Natalie said as she zipped up her coat.

"No. We figured it out an hour ago but we decided to tangle them up again since it was so much fun the first time," David replied with heavy sarcasm.

Natalie started for the door. "Well if it takes you much longer we'll be night fishing with a flashlight. Hopefully Mom and Dad will be back before then."

"Where are you going?"

"Just getting some more wood. The fire's almost out."

Natalie closed the front door and headed for the old pickup. She dumped two loads on the front steps and turned back to get a third when she saw Ben and Barb coming down the road holding hands.

"You guys get lost out there?" she yelled as she walked toward them.

Ben looked at Barb and smiled. "No, just hiking. You guys bored yet?"

"David and Greg have kept occupied with trying to untangle the fishing poles, but Liz and I are ready to do something. Anything!"

The three of them walked back to the pickup to grab some more wood. Once all the wood was in and the fire was crackling again, Ben called the four of them together. "Okay guys, we have about three hours of daylight left; what do you want to do?"

"Fish!"

"Hike!"

"Ski!"

"Okay, okay. I know you're all anxious to do something. How about I take who ever wants to go fishing down to the stream and Mom takes the others skiing?"

Greg grabbed one of the untangled poles and handed the other one to David.

"So you guys are going with me. Nat, Lizzy?"

"I kind of wanted to go on a hike," Natalie replied.

"We can do that tomorrow."

"Okay. Skiing it is."

"Me too," Liz agreed.

Ben and David lagged behind as Greg almost sprinted toward the stream trail. With the stream finally in sight David broke the silence, "So are you going to tell me what happened last night, or just Mom?"

"I'm going to tell you guys right now. Once we get our lines in the water."

The three of them found a perfect spot on the west side

of the stream. David and Greg put on a chunk of trout bait as Ben put on a rubber trout worm. Ben spread the thick blanket out on the snowy bank and the three anglers settled down to wait.

"Guys. I want to tell you something that is very important for you to hear. But first I want you to promise not to tell anyone else. I think you'll know why after I'm finished."

David glanced at Greg who had a puzzled look on his face.

"Greg, do you understand? I want your word that this will be our secret."

Greg nodded.

As the sun started to set and the shadows lengthened, Ben began to tell the boys about his encounter. For Greg's sake, he left out some of the deeper parts of the night's conversation, hoping to have a one-on-one with David at a later time.

Ben was almost finished when Greg blurted out, "So you didn't break the buddy rule!"

"Well, no, I guess I didn't, Greg. What could be more safe than hiking with an angel? But do you understand the importance of what Apokrin told me?"

"Yeah, I think so," Greg replied. "Grandpa's not really alone because God is with him. We can't always see that, but we're supposed to trust God, and you're nobody special, but God picked you anyway."

Ben and David both laughed.

"I think he understands, Dad."

"I guess so," Ben said. "But do…"

Ben's words were completely muffled by Greg's shouts as

he grabbed his pole and jerked it backwards while reeling it in. All three stood up as Greg slowly brought the fish out of the stream. Ben grabbed the end of the line and handed it to Greg, who by now was smiling ear to ear holding a fifteen-inch rainbow trout.

"One to nothing," Greg said as he put the trout in the bag. "I'm going to cream you guys this time."

chapter 24

Barb yelled at Natalie who was about twenty feet in front of her, "Tell Lizzy to stop. I need a rest!"

Natalie relayed the orders to her sister, and the three of them stopped at a clearing on the side of the ski trail. Barb stooped and took off one ski, and then the other. "I need to talk to you girls anyway," Barb struggled to get the words out between breaths.

The girls also popped their skis off and took a seat in the snow. Liz took off her back pack and rummaged through until she found three sandwiches and some chips. "I assume you guys are wondering why Dad and I went off on a hike earlier," Barb began after she had caught her breath.

"Yeah," Natalie replied. "And why Dad seems so tired."

"Well last night, for pretty much the whole night, Dad went on a hike."

"By himself! At night?!" Liz questioned.

"Yes at night. But not by himself."

Natalie and Liz gave each other a puzzled look and then turned back toward Barb who continued, "Dad told me all about it on our hike. What have we been praying about for the last year and a half more than anything else?"

"Grandpa Jake," Liz replied.

"Yes, Lizzy. And it appears after all this prayer God decided to answer us in a very special way. I know this is going to sound a bit odd, but last night…Dad went on a hike with an angel."

Both girls looked a bit stunned, but Barb thought she could see a hint of a smile on Lizzy's face. "That's why he is so tired—he didn't really sleep last night."

"So what did this angel say?" Natalie asked warily.

"I know it's hard to grasp. I had trouble at first, too. But your dad's not one to tell weird stories or lie to any of us, especially not something as important as this. As to what the angel said, it was, well, wonderful. He let Dad ask him questions about Grandpa's illness, among other things. It's probably best to let your dad tell you in person the specifics, but I can tell you a little bit now."

"Did he say that Grandpa would be healed?" Natalie asked.

Barb hesitated, then replied, "No."

Tears welled up in Natalie's eyes and Barb grabbed her hand. Liz put an arm around her. "Honey, it wasn't really about that. It seems that God sees things in a much deeper and purposeful way than we do. What the angel did tell Dad is that Grandpa is very much loved by God and not in any way abandoned by Him. In fact, he said that Jesus is with Grandpa right now in a better and more real way than any of us could imagine."

"But how?"

"I'm not sure, but the angel said we are supposed to trust in God's promises. The last words he said to Dad were those of Hebrews 13:5, 'Never will I leave you, never will I forsake you.' The angel assured Dad that Grandpa was taken care of and that our prayers matter."

"I knew that," Liz said as she popped a chip into her mouth. "Grandpa told me about that when he first got sick."

"He did?" Barb inquired.

"Yeah. He said, 'Never stop praying, and always remember that God will never leave you, no matter what.'"

"So that's what you meant when you said 'no matter what' to Grandpa every time we left the nursing home."

"Yeah, I guess. I just thought Grandpa knew what he was talking about."

"Well apparently he did," Barb said as she stood up. "Girls, it's starting to get dark. We better get our skis on and head back to the cabin."

The entire family enjoyed fresh fish for supper that night. Ben was sound asleep by nine o'clock and the rest of the family all turned in by 10:30 as they anticipated the long hike to Mystery Peak in the morning.

chapter 25

The sun was directly overhead when the seven of them turned the last corner on the trail and caught sight of the peak. A few hundred yards later they stripped off their backpacks and rested before having their picnic lunch with this spectacular view. Barb laid out the blanket and then took the large container of grapes out of her backpack. Everyone took their lunches out including a big slab of turkey lunch meat for Gabe. All of them bowed their heads as Ben prayed to give thanks for their food and their family.

As they began their lunch together they all looked at the beautiful scene around them. From Mystery Peak you could see plenty of other smaller snow covered peaks, thousands of trees, and hundreds of colors as the sunlight bounced off of the white snow.

As they sat and ate quietly, Barb broke the silence, "It sure is easy to believe in God when you see all of this."

"Yes, it is beautiful," Ben replied. "It was amazing at yesterday's sunrise too."

"What did the angel say about the view?" Liz asked.

"Honey, remember we agreed to let Daddy tell us about

the different parts of his talk with the angel when he saw fit," Barb gently corrected.

"Oh it's okay," Ben interrupted without taking his eyes off of the view. "It was really cool. He spent a long time just admiring it, soaking it in. He really seemed to enjoy it."

"But won't heaven be even cooler?" Greg asked.

"He said that this was just a very small glimpse of heaven, and he seemed to be emphasizing the 'very small.'"

All of them sat quietly again for a short moment. David then stood up and took a seat directly by his dad. "Dad, you said he talked about prayer, and how important it is. Did he tell you how it worked?"

"Not exactly, but he did tell me that God listens to every prayer, that He really likes hearing from us, that prayer is a gift, and that prayers are always answered—just not always answered in the way we would like.

The bottom line seemed to be two things—trust God, no matter what, and trust His word to us, no matter what."

The family talked a bit more about Apokrin's answers to Ben and finished up their lunch. They picked up their trash and food containers and stuffed them in to their backpacks. "Well, we better get going. We need to get back to the cabin so we can get home at a decent time tonight," Ben announced.

Each of the family members took one last look off of the peak and headed down the trail. Natalie hung back and lingered a bit longer. Barb started to turn around, but Ben urged her to go on. He turned around and walked back up the trail to where Natalie stood. As Ben came up beside her he could see that tears were streaming down her cheeks. "What's wrong Natalie?" he asked as he put his arm around her.

"I feel like such a jerk. All these months I've dreaded going to the nursing home. I never knew what to do, or what to say when I was there. Now I can see that I really wasn't worried about Grandpa, I was just worried about myself.'

Ben stood silent, sensing there was more.

"I guess God must be pretty disappointed in me right now."

Ben gave her a hug and then looked her in the eye. "Natalie, we all struggled with this. I felt much the same way you did through the whole thing. I keep wondering why God would choose me to send the angel to, and the only thing I could come back to was that I was the one He was disappointed in the most. I must have been the one that had the least amount of faith."

"You really think that?"

"Yeah, I really do. But you want to know the most amazing thing?"

Natalie started wiping the tears from her eyes and looked back at her dad, waiting.

"Even though I could see that there was some disappointment in Apokrin's voice at some of my questions, that was not the main feeling I got from him. What I got was a sense of how much God cared, how much God wanted to be more and more a part of people's lives. There may have been some disappointment, but certainly no condemnation. God knows our hearts. He knew that I still cared for Jake, that I wanted to do the right thing, but He knew I was looking in the wrong places too often."

"The wrong places?"

"Apokrin told me countless times that I was to know

God's word. I was told to always pray. I was told to make sure I always made time to worship and praise God together with other people; that God did not leave us without ways of coping; and to trust God, even when I don't completely understand what's going on. Natalie, God knows your heart and I know you too. You were struggling because you were dealing with something you didn't know how to handle. And I was no help to you. I went to see Jake less than you did."

"But you feel okay with all of this now?"

"I still don't know it all, Natalie. But I do trust in the One who does—and I know you do too. The Jesus we know may very well be disappointed in us, but He cares too much about us to turn His back on us. He's always available to work things out."

The tears had stopped and Natalie started heading down the trail. Ben immediately followed her, "You okay now?"

"Yeah," she said as she stopped and took one last look at the peak. "Do you think Apokrin will ever come to visit you again?"

"No. Definitely not."

"Definitely?"

"He said I would not see him again 'in this world.' I've thought about that a lot. We sort of became friends in that short time period. But with all his emphasis on God's word, prayer, and worship, I guess I should have enough to keep me trusting in God."

"He'll never leave us," Natalie said with a smile.

"Never."

chapter 26

"So you want to meet me at the nursing home at 4:30 tomorrow afternoon," Claire restated as she jotted the time down in her calendar book. She paused before hanging up. "Barb, I really think you should encourage Ben to come and see Dad too. I know he's having a really hard time with this, but I think it would be good if he would face it."

"He'll be there tomorrow," Barb replied as she balanced the phone between her neck and ear so she could put the toothpaste on her toothbrush.

"He will?"

"Yes. He's even leaving work early to pick up the two younger kids. We'll all be there at 4:30, Claire."

"All of you? Well, that's great. Did something happen up on that mountain this weekend?"

"Yes it did, but I'll let Ben tell you about that tomorrow. Good night." Barb pressed the off button on the phone and began brushing her teeth. *I wonder how much Ben will want to tell her,* she thought.

Claire closed her cell phone and began shutting the lights off in her apartment. "Ben's coming to see Dad tomorrow, and he has something to tell me about what happened on their camping trip," she whispered out loud, her mind racing as she wondered what this was all about. "I had a feeling something was going on with him."

Ben, Liz, and Greg met Barb and Natalie at the front door of the nursing home just before 4:30 Monday afternoon. As they headed down the hall towards Jake's room Barb glanced back. "Did you see David's car out there anywhere?"

"I didn't really look for it," Ben replied as they turned right and entered the room.

Claire was standing by the left side of the bed and David was seated in the window sill.

"Hey, bud, you made it," Ben said as he came over to David and slapped him on the back.

"Yeah. We're just supposed to go shoot at the gym from six to seven tonight."

Ben turned from the window and walked over to Jake's bed. He looked to Claire, "How's he doing today?"

"Oh pretty much the same—sure seems content though."

Ben took the seat at the side of the bed on Jake's right. He squeezed Jake's arm and looked into his eyes. "Dad, sorry for waiting so long between visits. I was so busy thinking about myself I forgot to think about you."

Claire slowly walked around the foot of the bed and joined the rest of the family gathered near the window.

Ben continued. "Jake, I had so many questions about why something like this would happen to you. We've all been praying a long time about this. You taught us all how important that is. This weekend, up at the cabin on the main trail, our prayers were answered. Jake, I know you are taken care of. I know that God is really with you right now. I still don't know why it has to be this way, but I now have the faith to trust that Jesus will take care of you—and all of us. I'm not sure if you can hear me right now, but I believe you know I'm here, and that it makes a difference. Barb and the kids are here too."

Ben motioned for the rest of the family to come over to the bed. Each one grabbed Jake's hand, part of his arm, or put their hand on his shoulder. "Can you feel that, Dad?" Ben said as they all looked at Jake's face. "You better get used to hearing my voice, because I'm going to be bugging you a lot more. I want to tell you all about a friend that I met on the mountain. Right now I'm going to pray for you."

The family bowed their heads as Ben prayed, "Heavenly Father, I just thank you that no matter how undeserving we sometimes are you still listen to our prayers and answer them. Thanks for answering all our prayers about Jake; for your promises to us and to him. Help us be faithful no matter what. Help us to trust you. Help us to remember your promise to never leave us or forsake us. In Jesus name, Amen."

For a moment, just a few seconds, all were silent. And from Jake's lips came the faint but clear words, "Never leave."

"Did you hear that?" Liz said as she broke the silence.

"Yeah!" Natalie agreed. "Grandpa said 'Never leave.'"

David looked at his mom who had a tear running down her cheek. He then turned to his dad who was now standing right next to him, "Hebrews 13:5. You just told us about that last night on the way home."

"Yeah, it's almost eerie isn't it?"

"I think it's cool," Natalie said as she put her arm around her dad.

Claire was soaking all of this in, but couldn't contain herself any longer. "So, just what did happen on that mountain, Ben?"

"Oh, Claire, you don't want to hear about any boring hiking stories do you?"

Claire shot back a steely glare.

"Okay, okay," Ben said, laughing. "Why don't you grab your coat and you and I can take a walk while the rest of the family spends some time with Dad. I'm sure you will have lots of questions and hopefully I can answer them."

"Go for a walk? It's cold out there! But I do have a number of questions for you!"

"Oh come on, Claire, a walk will help," Ben replied as the two headed out of the room.

"Help your answers?"

"Maybe. But I do think it will help your questions."